Table of Contents
Vocabulary Building
Grades

Different Languages	2
Nations of the World	4
Cities of the World	6
Famous Cities	8
Nations of the World	10
Nations of the World	12
Africa	14
Ancient Greece	16
Ancient Egypt	18
Acronyms and Abbreviations	20
Add an Adverb!	22
Preposition Position	24
Adjective Power	26
Adjective Power	28
Adjective Power	30
Spelling Challenge	32
Inventions of the World	34
Games and Sports	36
Making Music	38
Music to Our Ears	40
Color	42
Art	44
A World of Cats	46
A World of Dogs	48
Baby Animal Names	50
Male and Female Animals	52
Animal Groups	54
Grouping Interesting Animals	56
Incredible Insects	58
Reptiles of the Earth	60
Volcanoes	62
Light	64
Celestial Bodies	66
Constellations	68
Space Travel	70
The Space Shuttle	72
Computers	74
Computers	76
Polygons	78
Mathematics	80
Mathematic Terms	82

Different Languages

Place the languages listed in the Word Bank in alphabetical order.

1. _____
2. _____
3. _____
4. _____
5. _____
6. _____
7. _____
8. _____
9. _____
10. _____
11. _____
12. _____
13. _____
14. _____
15. _____
16. _____
17. _____
18. _____
19. _____

Word Bank

Norwegian	Icelandic	Italian	Danish
Portuguese	Spanish	Arabic	Greek
Tahitian	Russian	Polish	Hindi
Japanese	English	French	Thai
Mandarin	Swedish	German	

Write the language on the ladder rung next to the place where it spoken. The Word Bank will help you.

- Portugal
- northern India
- Mexico
- Poland
- Russia
- China
- Iceland
- Thailand
- Italy
- Sweden
- England
- Japan
- Norway
- Egypt
- Tahiti
- France
- Greece
- Denmark
- Germany

Nations of the World

Circle the nation that is not located on the same continent as the others listed in each group.

1. Sri Lanka, Thailand, Oman, Norway
2. Canada, United States, Mexico, West Germany
3. South Africa, Brazil, Morocco, Swaziland
4. Singapore, Zaire, Philippines, Saudi Arabia
5. Finland, Spain, American Samoa, France
6. Indonesia, Greece, China, Afghanistan
7. Japan, Iraq, Liberia, Israel
8. Belgium, Denmark, Austria, New Zealand
9. Afghanistan, Pakistan, China, Switzerland
10. Nigeria, Jordan, India, Kuwait
11. Singapore, Nepal, Zimbabwe, Afghanistan
12. Sweden, France, Fiji, Italy
13. Australia, Solomon Islands, New Zealand, Spain
14. Poland, Hungary, Peru, Norway
15. Uruguay, Italy, Denmark, Austria
16. Sweden, Venezuela, Luxembourg, Iceland
17. Greece, United States, Spain, Belgium
18. South Korea, India, Cameroon, Vietnam
19. Panama, Canada, Denmark, Guatemala
20. Bangladesh, Kenya, Jordan, Mongolia

Word Bank

West Germany	Philippines	Spain	Poland
Afghanistan	Thailand	China	Italy
New Zealand	Austria	Japan	Sweden
South Korea	France	U.S.S.R.	Greece
South Africa	Panama	India	Jordan

Write the name of the country on the ladder rung next to the type of money which is used there. The Word Bank will help you.

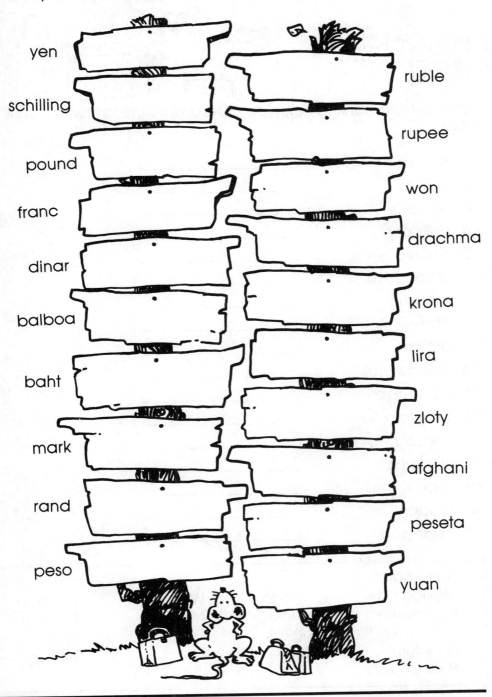

- yen
- schilling
- pound
- franc
- dinar
- balboa
- baht
- mark
- rand
- peso
- ruble
- rupee
- won
- drachma
- krona
- lira
- zloty
- afghani
- peseta
- yuan

Cities of the World

Use the Word Bank to help you unscramble the following list of cities.

1. bknasriaf _____
2. yyneds _____
3. eugarp _____
4. uulloonh _____
5. aailnm _____
6. vreocnvau _____
7. aammn _____
8. nbre _____
9. ddriam _____
10. xmeoci ytci _____
11. ddaahgb _____
12. aasntoig _____
13. wwaasr _____
14. kkognba _____
15. lami _____
16. ssaaun _____
17. haishgna _____

Word Bank

Mexico City	Santiago	Warsaw	Amman
Vancouver	Baghdad	Madrid	Nassau
Fairbanks	Bangkok	Prague	Lima
Honolulu	Sydney	Manila	Bern
Shanghai			

Write the name of a city from the Word Bank on the ladder rung next to the place where it is located.

Famous Cities

Use the Word Bank to help you unscramble the following list of cities.

1. npoecghaen _____
2. ooontrt _____
3. rjueasmel _____
4. eomr _____
5. sssleurb _____
6. nueosb rseia _____
7. lebmrouen _____
8. genbre _____
9. spria _____
10. xanealdrai _____
11. ouels _____
12. nnieav _____
13. edels _____
14. ppuasla _____
15. yookt _____
16. ndbiul _____
17. rtemdasam _____
18. slo gnaelse _____
19. kkviajyre _____

Word Bank

Buenos Aires	Alexandria	Uppsala	Tokyo
Melbourne	Jerusalem	Dublin	Paris
Copenhagen	Los Angeles	Vienna	Seoul
Amsterdam	Brussels	Bergen	Rome
Reykjavik	Toronto	Leeds	

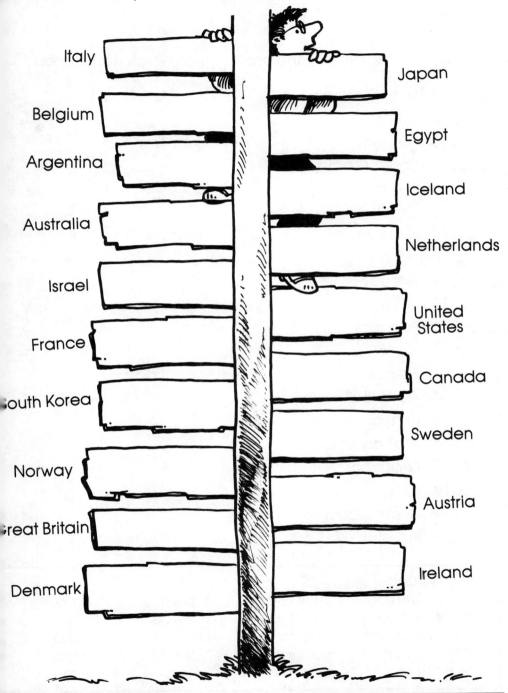

Nations of the World

Match each country with the continent on which it is located.

_____ 1. West Germany   A. North America
_____ 2. Iran
_____ 3. Turkey   B. South America
_____ 4. Saudi Arabia
_____ 5. Sweden   C. Asia
_____ 6. China
_____ 7. Yugoslavia   D. Europe
_____ 8. India
_____ 9. Greece   E. Africa
_____ 10. Bolivia
_____ 11. Portugal   F. Australia
_____ 12. Norway
_____ 13. Finland   G. Antarctica
_____ 14. Australia
_____ 15. Kenya
_____ 16. Afghanistan
_____ 17. Lebanon
_____ 18. Syria
_____ 19. Great Britain
_____ 20. Egypt

Word Bank

Great Britain	Australia	Turkey	Syria
West Germany	Lebanon	Greece	China
Saudi Arabia	Bolivia	Finland	India
Afghanistan	Portugal	Norway	Egypt
Yugoslavia	Sweden	Kenya	Iran

Write the name of the country on the ladder rung next to its capital. The Word Bank will help you.

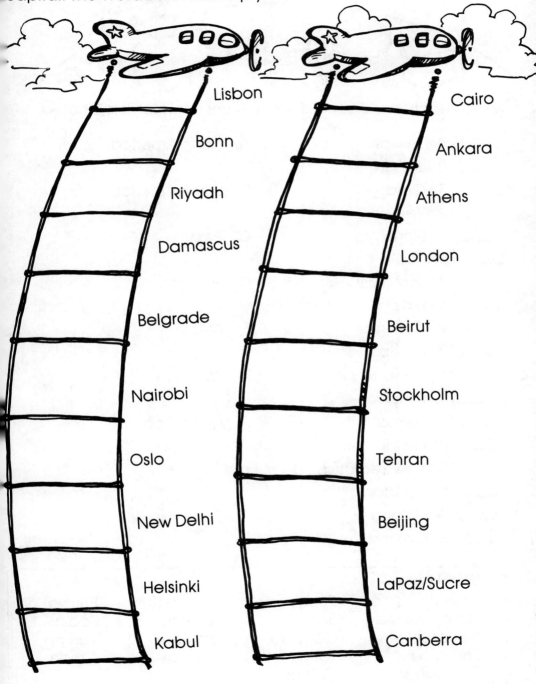

Nations of the World

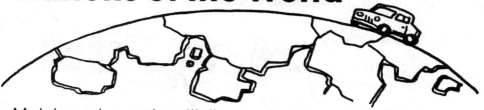

Match each country with the continent on which it is located.

_____ 1. Taiwan   A. North America

_____ 2. Japan

_____ 3. Oman   B. South America

_____ 4. Yemen

_____ 5. Norway   C. Asia

_____ 6. Spain

_____ 7. Jamaica   D. Europe

_____ 8. Brazil

_____ 9. Canada   E. Africa

_____ 10. Mexico

_____ 11. Venezuela   F. Australia

_____ 12. Ecuador

_____ 13. Burma   G. Antarctica

_____ 14. Philippines

_____ 15. New Zealand

_____ 16. Pakistan

_____ 17. Finland

_____ 18. Iceland

Word Bank

Philippines	Ecuador	Iceland	Burma
New Zealand	Brazil	Mexico	Spain
Venezuela	Canada	Japan	Yemen
Jamaica	Taiwan	Norway	Oman
Pakistan	Finland		

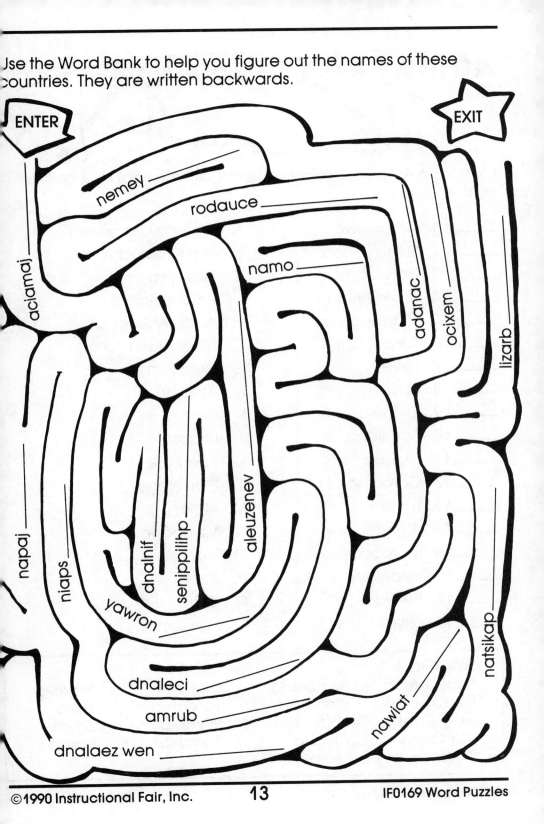

Africa

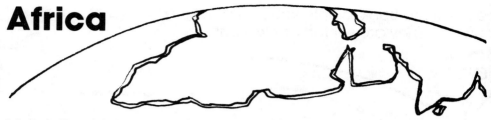

Match the African nations on the left with their capitals on the right.

_____ 1. Zimbabwe	A. Pretoria/Capetown
_____ 2. Sierra Leone	B. Dar es Salaam
_____ 3. Ivory Coast	C. Kinshasa
_____ 4. South Africa	D. Antananarivo
_____ 5. Madagascar	E. Addis Ababa
_____ 6. Tanzania	F. Mogadishu
_____ 7. Zaire	G. Freetown
_____ 8. Somalia	H. Abidjan
_____ 9. Ethiopia	I. Harare
_____ 10. Botswana	J. Lagos
_____ 11. Nigeria	K. Yaoundé
_____ 12. Cameroon	L. Gaborone
_____ 13. Tunisia	M. Algiers
_____ 14. Algeria	N. Mbabane
_____ 15. Morocco	O. Tunis
_____ 16. Swaziland	P. Rabat
_____ 17. Kenya	Q. Cairo
_____ 18. Egypt	R. Nairobi

Word Bank

South Africa	Swaziland	Tunisia	Nigeria
Sierra Leone	Cameroon	Tanzania	Zaire
Ivory Coast	Botswana	Ethiopia	Egypt
Madagascar	Algeria	Somalia	Kenya
Zimbabwe	Morocco		

©1990 Instructional Fair, Inc.   IF0169 Word Puzzles

Ancient Greece

Use the Word Bank to help you unscramble the following terms about ancient Greece.

1. idila _____
2. rmeoh _____
3. yphooslpih _____
4. etlotsira _____
5. setarcohpip _____
6. pcmiylo sgmae _____
7. nnoehtrap _____
8. slioporca _____
9. seallh _____
10. nsehta _____
11. aotlp _____
12. taesrcso _____
13. aaelyppor _____
14. yyssedo _____
15. aadecym _____
16. plahteba _____
17. eeruak _____
18. nothaarm _____

Word Bank

Olympic Games	Acropolis	Odyssey	Plato
Hippocrates	Parthenon	academy	Hellas
philosophy	Socrates	eureka	Homer
Aristotle	alphabet	Athens	Iliad
Propylaea	marathon		

Use the Word Bank to help you figure out these ancient Greek terms. They are written backwards.

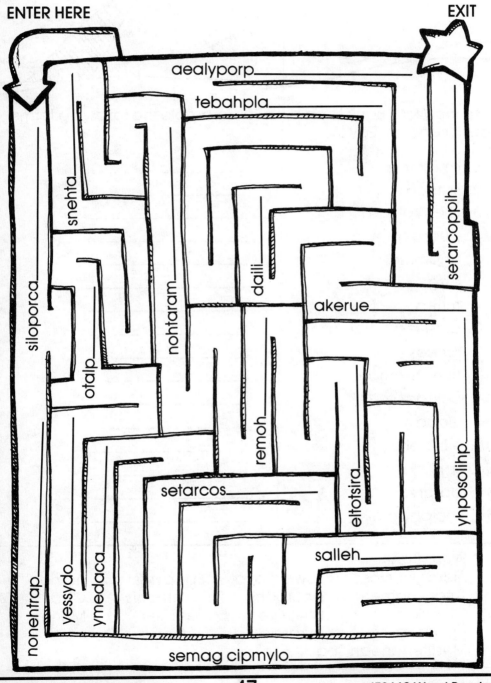

Ancient Egypt

Use the Word Bank to help you unscramble the following terms about ancient Egypt.

1. smidrypa _____
2. sstteea _____
3. roewl ptyge _____
4. pupre gepyt _____
5. sihpmme _____
6. aizg _____
7. mneo _____
8. dmetiearrnnae ase _____
9. nmees _____
10. ttunahknmae _____
11. oelcaaptr _____
12. rficaa _____
13. eiln rreiv _____
14. sphhaaor _____
15. ppsurya _____
16. shcipgyloreih _____

Word Bank

hieroglyphics	Lower Egypt	papyrus	nome
Tutankhamen	pharoahs	Memphis	Giza
Cleopatra	Nile River	estates	Menes
Upper Egypt	pyramids	Africa	
Mediterranean Sea			

Use the Word Bank to help you figure out these Egyptian terms. They are written backwards.

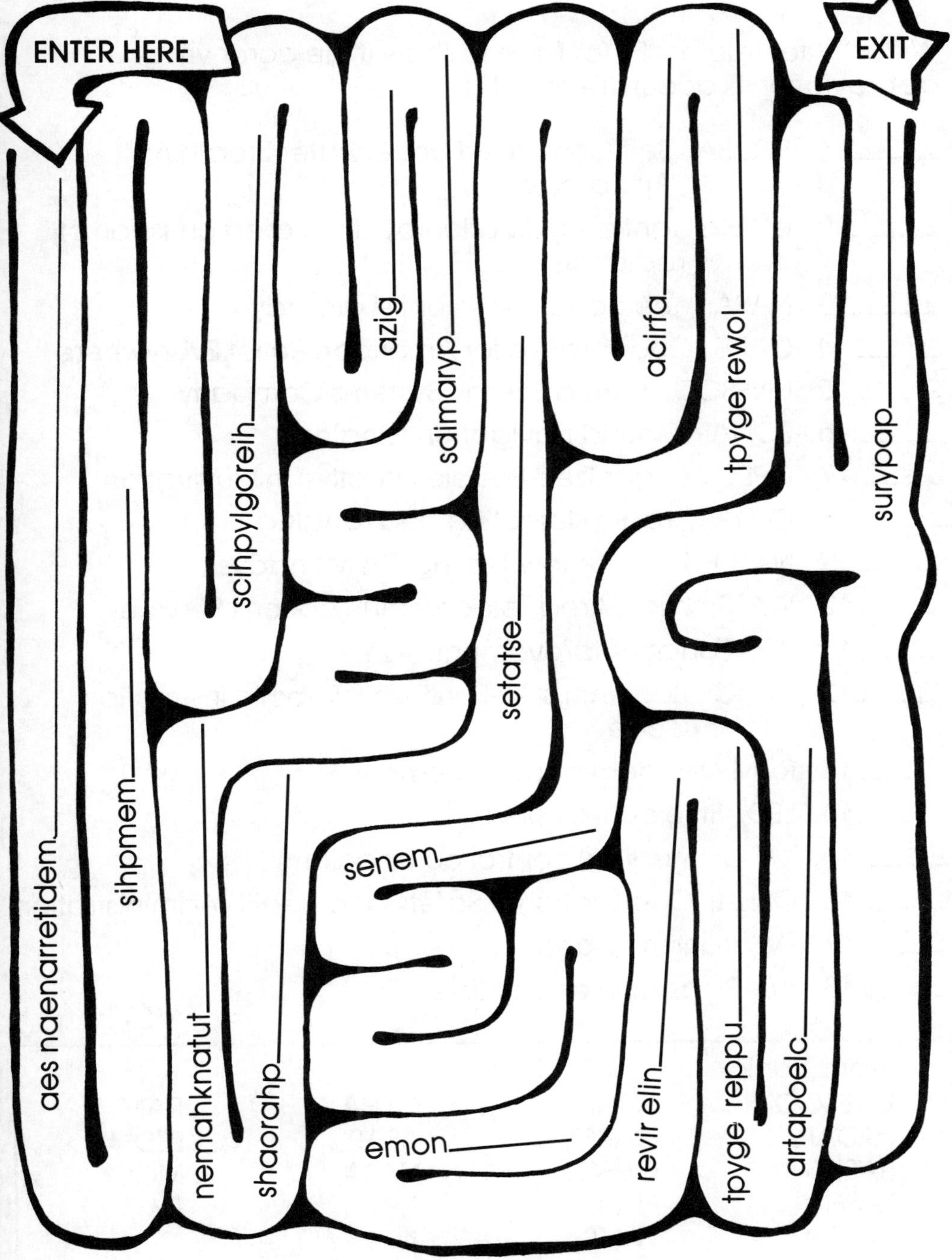

ENTER HERE
EXIT

- azig
- sdimaryp
- acirfa
- tpyge rewol
- scihpylgoreih
- surypap
- setatse
- senem
- sihpmem
- aes naenarretidem
- nemahknatut
- shaorahp
- emon
- revir elin
- tpyge reppu
- artapoelc

Acronyms and Abbreviations

Write "T" for true or "F" for false to show if the acronym or abbreviation is accurate or not.

_____ 1. SCUBA: Self-Contained Underwater Breathing Apparatus

_____ 2. LASER: light amplification by stimulated emission of radiation

_____ 3. NASA: need another scientist already

_____ 4. CARE: Cooperative for American Relief Everywhere

_____ 5. UNESCO: United Energy Systems Company

_____ 6. SONAR: sound navigation ranging

_____ 7. OPEC: Organized People Effective In Cultivation

_____ 8. RADAR: radio detecting and ranging

_____ 9. NATO: Never Allow Testing On Mondays

_____ 10. WATS: Wide-Area Telecommunications Service

_____ 11. ZIP: Zoning Improvement Plan

_____ 12. BASIC: Beginner's All-Purpose Symbolic Instruction Code

_____ 13. RAM: random access memory

_____ 14. LED: little energy drive

_____ 15. MCC: medical control companion

_____ 16. OSHA: Occupational Safety and Health Administration

_____ 17. TV: transmit video

_____ 18. ASAP: as slow as possible

Word Bank

UNESCO	SONAR	OSHA	RAM
RADAR	CARE	ASAP	LED
BASIC	OPEC	NASA	MCC
LASER	NATO	ZIP	TV
SCUBA	WATS		

Use the Word Bank to help you figure out these acronyms and abbreviations. They are written backwards.

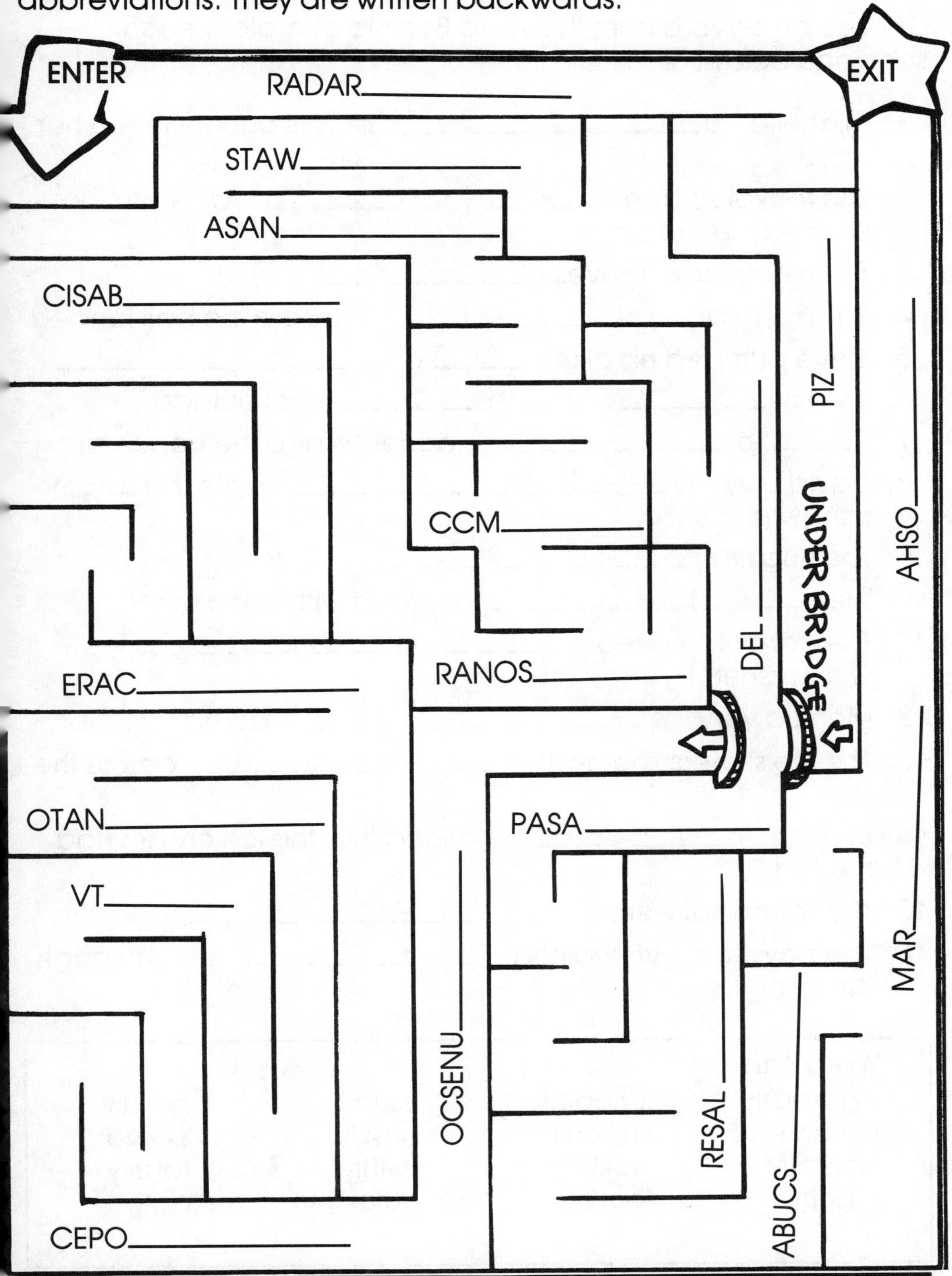

ENTER

EXIT

RADAR

STAW

ASAN

CISAB

PIZ

CCM

UNDER BRIDGE

AHSO

DEL

ERAC

RANOS

OTAN

PASA

VT

MAR

OCSENU

RESAL

ABUCS

CEPO

Add an Adverb!

Choose an adverb from the Word Bank to complete each sentence below.

1. Michelle u _ _ _ _ _ _ orders anchovies on her pizza.
2. The rocket zoomed _ _ y _ _ _ _ as Andy pushed the button.
3. The newspaper arrives _ _ _ l _.
4. Sam ran q _ _ _ _ _ _ to where the ball landed.
5. Steve pumped his bike _ _ g _ _ _ _ _ _ _.
6. It was _ _ _ _ _ m _ _ _ hot outside.
7. " _ _ p _ _ _ _ _ done!" yelled the coach.
8. David only p _ _ _ _ _ _ _ ate the sardine sandwich.
9. The ring fit l _ _ _ _ _ _.
10. We _ _ t _ _ _ _ agreed with each other.
11. The car only moved _ _ _ g _ _ _ _ as the wind rushed by.
12. Monica very p _ _ _ _ _ _ _ asked for help.
13. The ice skaters zoomed s _ _ _ _ _ _ across the ice.
14. Eva _ a _ _ _ _ noticed that the ice cream had melted.
15. The rehearsal went _ m _ _ _ _ _ _.
16. The boys and girls walked _ r _ _ _ _ _ through the rain.

Word Bank

vigorously	smoothly	usually	hardly
extremely	superbly	briskly	skyward
partially	politely	swiftly	totally
slightly	loosely	quickly	daily

©1990 Instructional Fair, Inc.   IF0169 Word Puzzles

Unscramble the letters to spell adverbs. The Word Bank will help you.

- OTYHLMOS
- POLITELY
- KYSRDWA
- LYOOSEL
- LYALOTT
- SERDWA (KYSRDWA)
- IDLADY
- LYHARD
- GOVILYRUS
- FTSWILY
- LYUICQK
- EMELYTR
- RYALPATI
- LYPESRBU
- YLLUSUA
- SLHTLLYIG
- ISBRLYK

23 IF0169 Word Puzzles

Preposition Position

"OUTSIDE THE DOOR, PLEASE."

Complete each sentence with a preposition from the Word Bank.

1. We decided to walk all the way a _ _ _ _ _ the lake.
2. A _ _ _ _ _ the lake we could see three large eagles!
3. The football rolled b _ _ _ _ _ the porch.
4. The baby giraffe followed b _ _ _ _ us.
5. The monkey would not come n _ _ _ us.
6. They all leaned their guitars a _ _ _ _ _ the amplifier.
7. The ball landed o _ _ _ _ _ _ of the ball park.
8. David gently placed the chameleon u _ _ _ the table.
9. They spotted the warthog just b _ _ _ _ _ the ridge.
10. We saw birds t _ _ _ _ _ _ _ _ the entire hike.
11. Have you ever been i _ _ _ _ _ a submarine?
12. You should not talk loudly d _ _ _ _ _ the movie.

Word Bank

throughout	around	beyond	inside
beneath	outside	during	near
against	across	behind	upon

Adjective Power

Circle the word in each row that is spelled correctly.

1. luckszurious — luxszurious — luxurious
2. contagious — kontagous — contagous
3. uneek — unique — youneek
4. ambitious — ambishous — ambishus
5. gigantic — jigantic — jygantic
6. occasional — okayzional — okaysionul
7. empresseve — empresive — impressive
8. humurus — humuraus — humorous
9. supearier — superior — souperior
10. furocious — ferocious — furohshus
11. vigurus — vigorous — veegurous
12. misteareus — mysterious — misteryous

Word Bank
mysterious   luxurious   impressive   superior
contagious   ambitious   humorous   vigorous
occasional   ferocious   gigantic   unique

Unscramble the letters to spell adjectives. The Word Bank will help you.

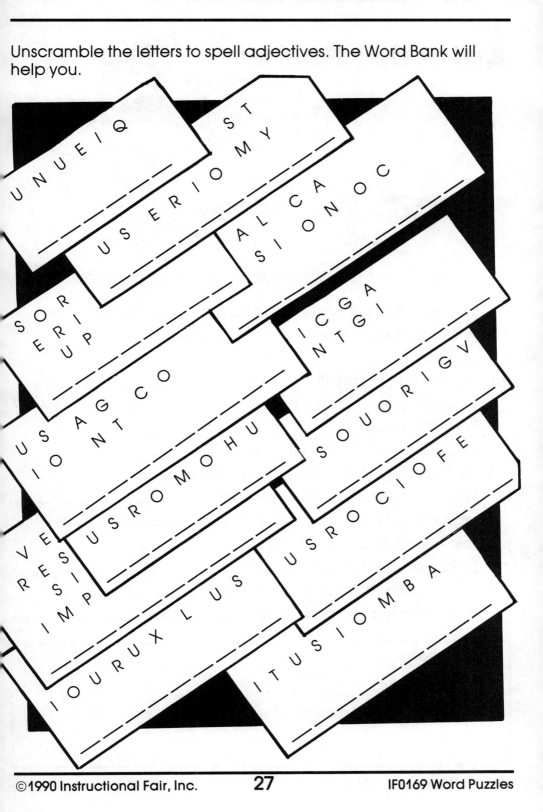

Adjective Power

Use adjectives from the Word Bank to complete each analogy.

1. Whimper is to sob, as _____ is to movable.
2. Fabulous is to wonderful, as creative is to _____.
3. Positive is to negative, as unbreakable is to _____.
4. Past is to future, as tiny is to _____.
5. Gnaw is to chew, as shakey is to _____.
6. Soothe is to comfort, as authentic is to _____.
7. Typical is to unusual, as cheerful is to _____.
8. Vapor is to mist, as sudden is to _____.
9. Join is to quit, as thin is to _____.
10. Solid is to liquid, as useless is to _____.
11. Poor is to wealthy, as lean is to _____.
12. Vow is to promise, as smart is to _____.

Word Bank

intelligent	portable	rickety	thick
inventive	immense	fragile	abrupt
effective	genuine	dreary	stout

Unscramble the letters to spell adjectives. The Word Bank will help you.

FEEFVECTI
_____

LE RAFGI
_____

ICRTYKE
_____

ABPTRU
_____

TCKHI
_____

VE IENNVTI
_____

ENNEUIG
_____

GE NT NT ELILI
_____

UTTOS
_____

DRRYEA
_____

MMISEEN
_____

LERTABPO
_____

Adjective Power

Match each adjective with its synonym.

_____ 1. absurd   A. bendable
_____ 2. elaborate   B. genuine
_____ 3. brief   C. ridiculous
_____ 4. precise   D. quick
_____ 5. breathtaking   E. fancy
_____ 6. flexible   F. strange
_____ 7. authentic   G. stunning
_____ 8. frail   H. fragile
_____ 9. reliable   I. exact
_____10. humble   J. many
_____11. numerous   K. dainty
_____12. peculiar   L. dependable
_____13. delicate   M. modest

Word Bank

breathtaking	reliable	delicate	absurd
elaborate	numerous	precise	brief
authentic	peculiar	humble	frail
flexible			

Unscramble the letters to spell adjectives. The Word Bank will help you.

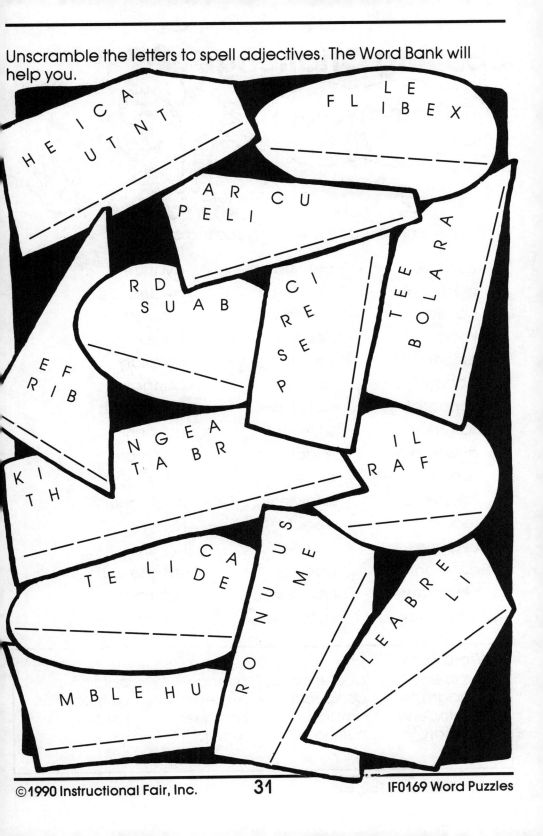

Spelling Challenge

Circle the word in each row that is spelled correctly.

1.	avanew	avenue	avanue
2.	awdiance	audience	awdeance
3.	caution	cawshon	kawtion
4.	knob	nobb	nawb
5.	simplify	simplafi	cimplafy
6.	banqwit	banquet	bangqwit
7.	awtograf	autograph	awtograph
8.	safishent	sufficient	saficient
9.	evaporate	evaparate	ivaporate
10.	seeze	cieze	seize
11.	fotogenic	fotowjenic	photogenic
12.	receet	reseate	receipt
13.	hygiene	higene	hijean
14.	genuien	genuine	jenuine
15.	newtrishus	newtreshus	nutritious
16.	conductor	kunducter	cunducter

Word Bank

sufficient	audience	avenue	caution
autograph	conductor	hygiene	genuine
photogenic	simplify	banquet	knob
evaporate	nutritious	receipt	seize

Write each word from the Word Bank in alphabetical order.

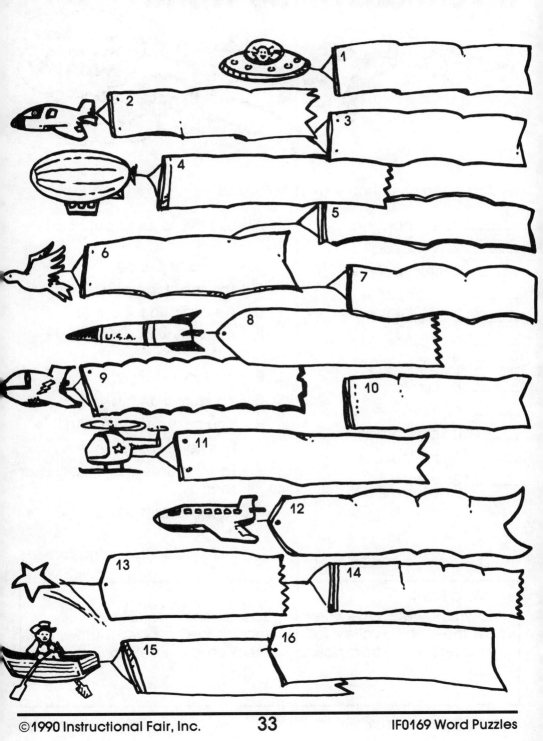

Inventions of the World

Match each invention with its definition.

_____ 1. saxophone
_____ 2. volleyball
_____ 3. trampoline
_____ 4. margarine
_____ 5. parachute
_____ 6. crossword
_____ 7. typewriter
_____ 8. airplane
_____ 9. lawn mower
_____ 10. basketball
_____ 11. synthesizer
_____ 12. velcro

A. Use this to jump out of an airplane
B. A kind of puzzle
C. This machine prints words
D. A substitute for butter
E. A game with a ball and a net
F. A wind instrument
G. You jump on this
H. You cut your lawn with this
I. This holds things shut
J. This instrument imitates other sounds
K. A game with a ball and hoop
L. Ride inside this in the air

Word Bank
lawn mower   typewriter   saxophone   airplane
synthesizer volleyball   margarine   parachute
basketball   trampoline   crossword   velcro

Write each invention from the Word Bank in alphabetical order.

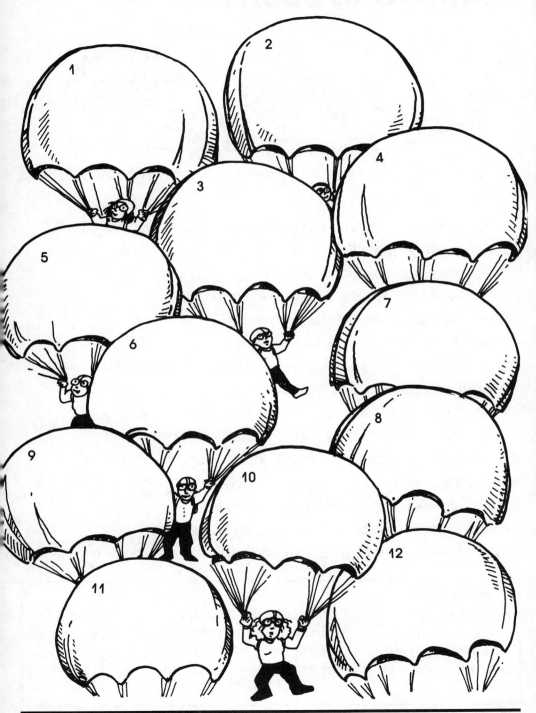

Games and Sports

Circle the word or phrase that does not belong in each category.

1. horseshoes: ringers, shoulder pads, metal stakes, "clank!"
2. Ping-Pong: paddles, little net, serve, "slam dunk!"
3. ice-skating: steel blades, ball, gliding, ice
4. waterskiing: boats, skis, water, face masks
5. tetherball: pole, referee, rope, hit
6. kickball: pitcher, mit, bases, ball
7. volleyball: net, serve, catch, volley
8. softball: mit, kick, outfield, catcher
9. football: quarterback, racket, touchdown, field goal
10. basketball: basket, tackle, dribbling, "slam dunk!"
11. soccer: goalkeepers, hoop, kick, bounce
12. surfing: wax, boat, surfboard, waves
13. tennis: net, bat, rackets, tennis balls
14. ice hockey: puck, ice skates, cage, sled
15. croquet: mallets, wire wickets, horseshoes, wooden balls

Word Bank			
Ping-Pong	tetherball	kickball	tennis
waterskiing	ice hockey	softball	surfing
ice-skating	horseshoes	football	soccer
basketball	volleyball	croquet	

Write each game from the Word Bank in alphabetical order.

Making Music

Circle the word in each row that is spelled correctly.

1. trambown / trawmbone / trombone
2. kastinetts / castinets / castanets
3. tamboreen / tambourine / tamborene
4. claranet / clarinet / clairanet
5. violen / violyn / violin
6. chello / chellow / cello
7. trumpit / trumpitt / trumpet
8. fluut / fluat / flute
9. harpsacord / harpsichord / harpsakord
10. gatar / getar / guitar
11. xylophone / zilafone / zilaphone
12. glockinspheel / glockenspiel / glockenspeel

Word Bank

glockenspiel, castanets, clarinet, violin
harpsichord, trombone, trumpet, cello
tambourine, xylophone, guitar, flute

Write each musical instrument from the Word Bank in alphabetical order.

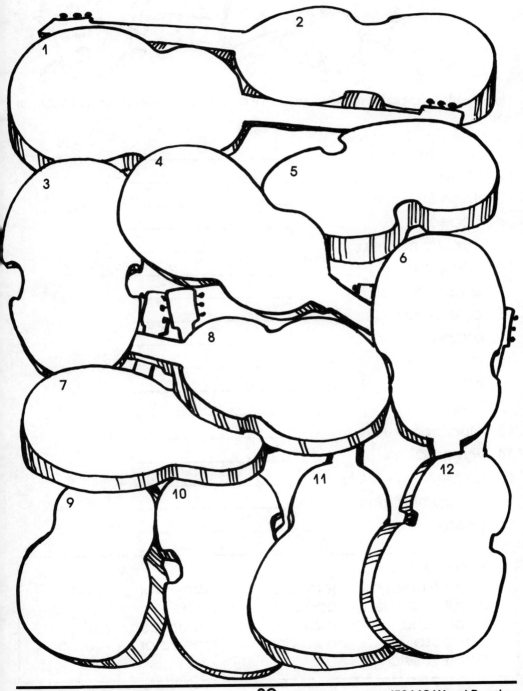

Music to Our Ears

Use the Word Bank to help you unscramble the following musical terms.

1. aatmrfe _____
2. ntrapssoe _____
3. ltnao smiuc _____
4. dcaeenc _____
5. lcasuim ttoannoi _____
6. hcrosetar _____
7. smcianyd _____
8. pesromoc _____
9. otmpe _____
10. ntoaal scium _____
11. htcip _____
12. lyets _____
13. etno loocr _____
14. yhmnora _____
15. ldyoem _____
16. ccoapmnaimnet _____
17. dhcro _____

Word Bank
musical notation   fermata   composer   style
accompaniment   cadence   orchestra   chord
tonal music   melody   dynamics   pitch
transpose   harmony   tone color tempo
atonal music

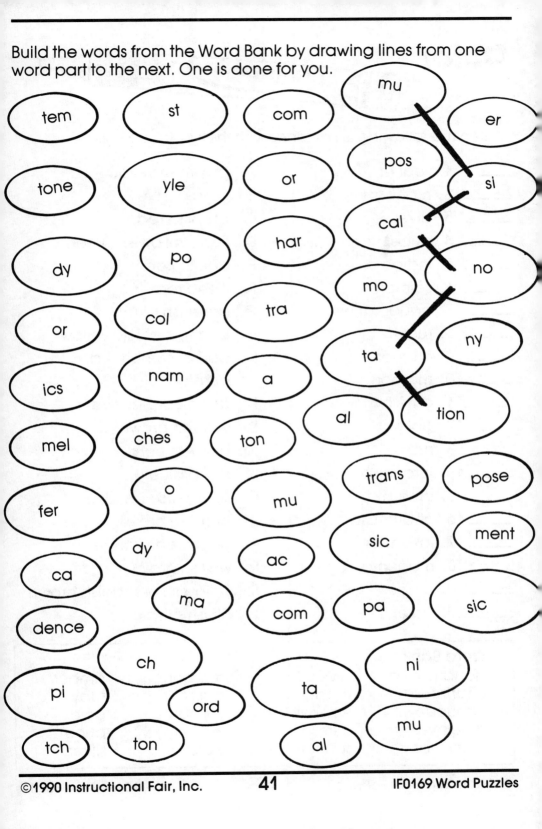

Color

Match the following list of tones with their color definitions.

_____ 1. scarlet
_____ 2. mahogany
_____ 3. silver
_____ 4. puce
_____ 5. indigo
_____ 6. salmon
_____ 7. aquamarine
_____ 8. russet
_____ 9. crimson
_____ 10. maroon
_____ 11. amethyst
_____ 12. gold
_____ 13. ruby
_____ 14. turquoise
_____ 15. emerald
_____ 16. chartreuse
_____ 17. lavender
_____ 18. magenta
_____ 19. amber
_____ 20. violet

A. brownish yellow
B. pale purple
C. purplish red
D. light, yellowish-green
E. deep green
F. deep red
G. greenish blue
H. bright, metallic yellow
I. dark brownish red
J. purple
K. deep purplish red
L. reddish brown
M. bluish green
N. deep blue
O. light yellowish-pink
P. purplish brown
Q. bright red-orange
R. whitish gray
S. yellowish or reddish brown
T. bluish purple

Word Bank

aquamarine	lavender	maroon	amber
chartreuse	magenta	russet	ruby
turquoise	emerald	salmon	gold
amethyst	crimson	indigo	puce
mahogany	scarlet	violet	silver

TUTOR'S GUIDE

Vocabulary Building with Word Puzzles
Grades 6-8

©1990 Instructional Fair, Inc.

IF0169 Tutor's Guide

The Tutor's Guide has been placed in the center of this homework booklet so that it can be easily removed.

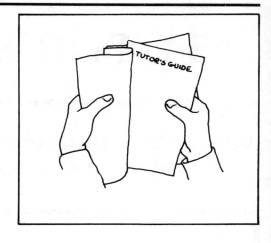

*A motivational award is provided on the inside back cover. It has been designed to be signed by the tutor.

The answer pages begin here. To simplify checking, they reflect the layout of the booklet pages.

©1990 Instructional Fair, Inc.

IF0169 Tutor's Guide

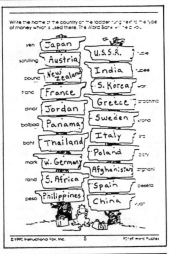
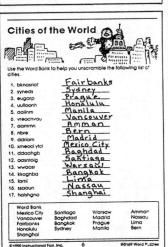

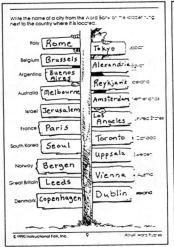

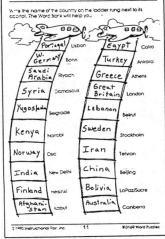

©1990 Instructional Fair, Inc.

IF0169 Tutor's Guide

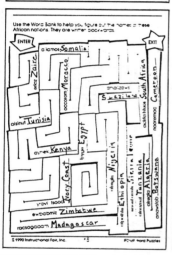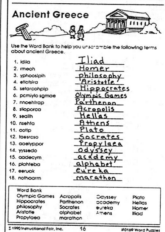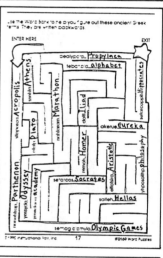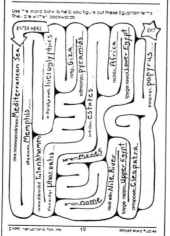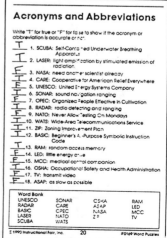

©1990 Instructional Fair, Inc.   IF0169 Tutor's Guide

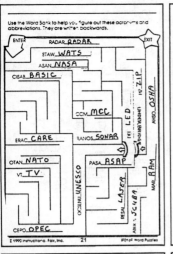
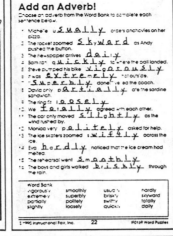
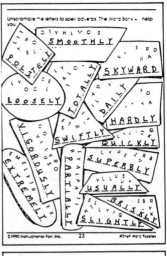

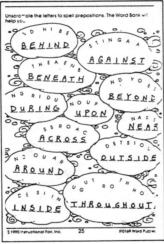
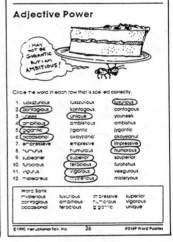
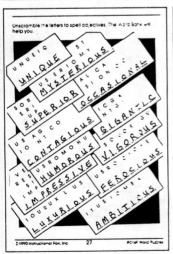
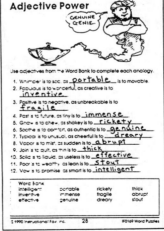

©1990 Instructional Fair, Inc.

IF0169 Tutor's Guide

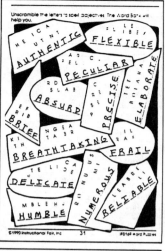
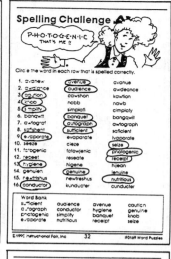
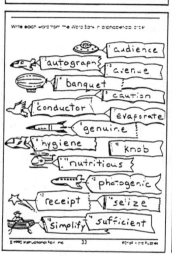

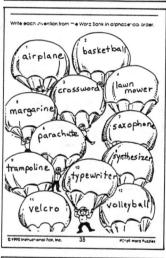

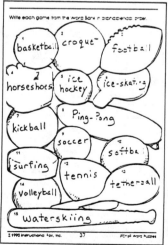

©1990 Instructional Fair, Inc. IF0169 Tutor's Guide

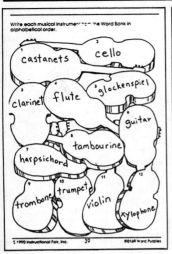

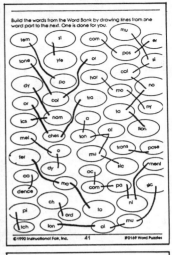

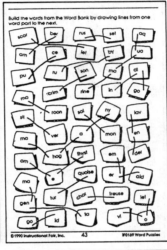
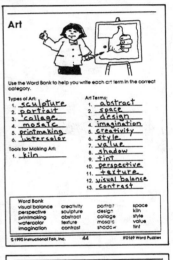

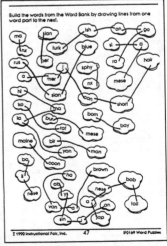

IF0169 Tutor's Guide

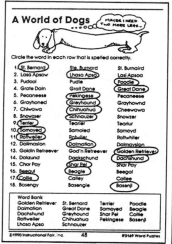
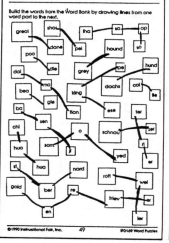

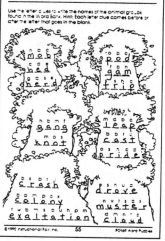
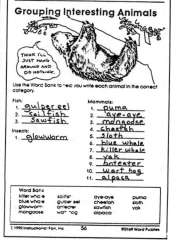

©1990 Instructional Fair, Inc.   IF0169 Tutor's Guide

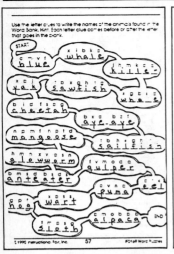

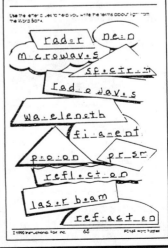

©1990 Instructional Fair, Inc.   IF0169 Tutor's Guide

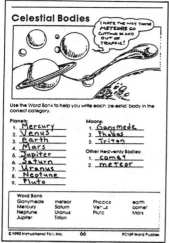
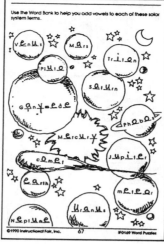

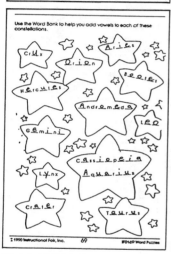

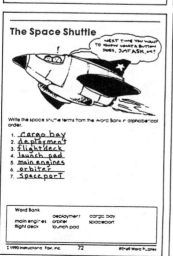

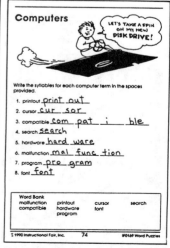

©1990 Instructional Fair, Inc. IF0169 Tutor's Guide

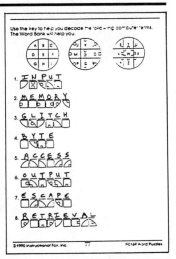
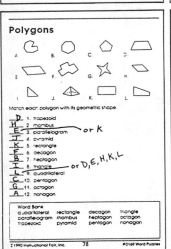
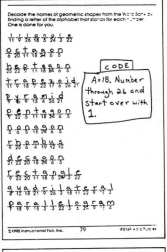

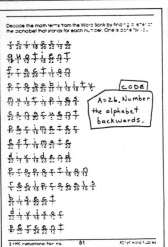
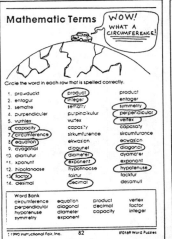

©1990 Instructional Fair, Inc.

IF0169 Tutor's Guide

Build the words from the Word Bank by drawing lines from one word part to the next.

Art

Use the Word Bank to help you write each art term in the correct category.

Types of Art:
1. _____
2. _____
3. _____
4. _____
5. _____
6. _____

Tools for Making Art:
1. _____

Art Terms:
1. _____
2. _____
3. _____
4. _____
5. _____
6. _____
7. _____
8. _____
9. _____
10. _____
11. _____
12. _____
13. _____

Word Bank

visual balance	creativity	portrait	space
perspective	sculpture	design	kiln
printmaking	abstract	collage	style
watercolor	texture	mosaic	value
imagination	contrast	shadow	tint

Build the words from the Word Bank by drawing lines from one word part to the next.

A World of Cats

Write the different breeds of cats from the Word Bank in alphabetical order.

1. _____
2. _____
3. _____
4. _____
5. _____
6. _____
7. _____
8. _____
9. _____
10. _____
11. _____
12. _____
13. _____
14. _____
15. _____
16. _____
17. _____

Word Bank

American Shorthair   Himalayan   Balinese   Manx
Japanese Bobtail   Abyssinian   Burmese   Korat
Turkish Angora   Maine Coon   Persian   Sphynx
Russian Blue   Siamese   Bombay   Birman
Havana Brown

Build the words from the Word Bank by drawing lines from one word part to the next.

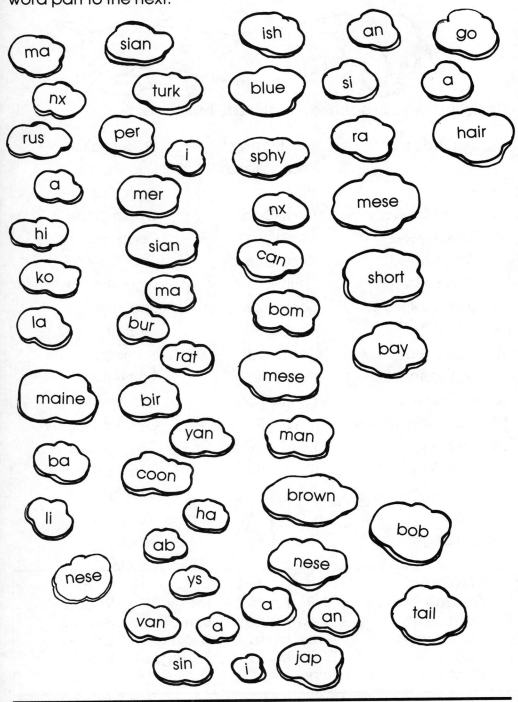

A World of Dogs

Circle the word in each row that is spelled correctly.

1. St. Bernard / Ste. Burnard / St. Burnaird
2. Lasa Apsow / Lhasa Apso / Lasi Apsoa
3. Pudool / Pudle / Poodle
4. Grate Dain / Grait Dane / Great Dane
5. Pecaneese / Pekingese / Pecaneese
6. Grayhoned / Greyhound / Grayhownd
7. Chiwawa / Chihuahua / Cheewawa
8. Snowzser / Schnauzer / Snowzer
9. Terrier / Tearier / Teariur
10. Samoyed / Samoied / Samoyd
11. Rottweiler / Rotwiler / Rottwhiler
12. Dallmasion / Dalmatian / Dalmaysion
13. Goldin Retreever / God'n Retreever / Golden Retriever
14. Dakzund / Dackschund / Dachshund
15. Char Pay / Shar Pei / Shar Pay
16. Beegul / Beagle / Beegal
17. Collie / Calley / Callee
18. Basengy / Basengie / Basenji

Word Bank
Golden Retriever St. Bernard Terrier Poodle
Dalmatian Great Dane Samoyed Beagle
Dachshund Greyhound Shar Pei Collie
Rottweiler Chihuahua Pekingese Basenji
Lhasa Apso Schnauzer

Build the words from the Word Bank by drawing lines from one word part to the next.

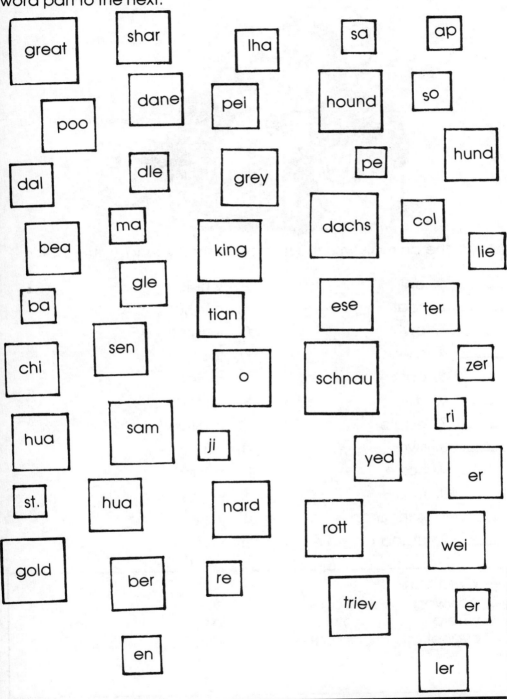

Baby Animal Names

Match the animals with the names for their young.

_____ 1. eel   A. whelp
_____ 2. seal   B. cygnet
_____ 3. owl   C. eaglet
_____ 4. sheep   D. foal
_____ 5. cow   E. owlet
_____ 6. dog   F. lamb
_____ 7. eagle   G. polliwog
_____ 8. swan   H. calf
_____ 9. horse   I. pup
_____ 10. frog   J. squab
_____ 11. kangaroo   K. joey
_____ 12. pigeon   L. elver

Word Bank

polliwog	eaglet	calf	lamb
whelp	owlet	joey	foal
cygnet	squab	elver	pup

Use the letter clues to write the names of baby animals found in the Word Bank. Hint: Each letter clue comes before or after the letter that goes in the blank.

Male and Female Animals

Match the animals with their gender names.

_____ 1. male bobcat
_____ 2. female tiger
_____ 3. male antelope
_____ 4. female fox
_____ 5. female lion
_____ 6. female cat
_____ 7. male goose
_____ 8. female elephant
_____ 9. male sheep
_____ 10. female swan
_____ 11. male horse
_____ 12. male duck

A. drake
B. stallion
C. ram
D. pen
E. cow
F. queen
G. gander
H. lioness
I. vixen
J. tigress
K. buck
L. tom

Word Bank

stallion	gander	drake	ram
tigress	vixen	buck	pen
lioness	queen	tom	cow

Use the letter clues to write the names of the animals found in the Word Bank. Hint: Each letter clue comes before or after the letter that goes in the blank.

Animal Groups

Place the animal group names from the Word Bank in alphabetical order.

1. _____
2. _____
3. _____
4. _____
5. _____
6. _____
7. _____
8. _____
9. _____
10. _____
11. _____
12. _____
13. _____
14. _____
15. _____
16. _____
17. _____

Word Bank

exaltation	drove	herd	gam
muster	cloud	trip	bed
colony	knot	leap	pod
pride	gang	cast	mob
crash			

Use the letter clues to write the names of the animal groups found in the Word Bank. Hint: Each letter clue comes before or after the letter that goes in the blank.

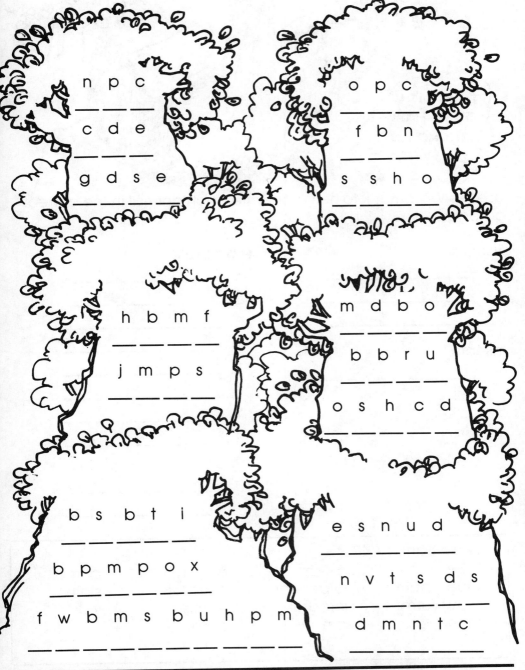

Grouping Interesting Animals

Use the Word Bank to help you write each animal in the correct category.

Fish:
1. _____
2. _____
3. _____

Insects:
1. _____

Mammals:
1. _____
2. _____
3. _____
4. _____
5. _____
6. _____
7. _____
8. _____
9. _____
10. _____
11. _____

Word Bank

killer whale	sailfish	aye-aye	puma
blue whale	gulper eel	cheetah	sloth
glowworm	anteater	sawfish	yak
mongoose	wart hog	alpaca	

Use the letter clues to write the names of the animals found in the Word Bank. Hint: Each letter clue comes before or after the letter that goes in the blank.

Incredible Insects

Write the insect names from the Word Bank in alphabetical order.

1. _____
2. _____
3. _____
4. _____
5. _____
6. _____
7. _____
8. _____
9. _____
10. _____
11. _____
12. _____
13. _____
14. _____

Word Bank

grasshopper	butterfly	ladybug	punkie
silverfish	stinkbug	katydid	cicada
dragonfly	termite	firefly	moth
mealworm	lacewing		

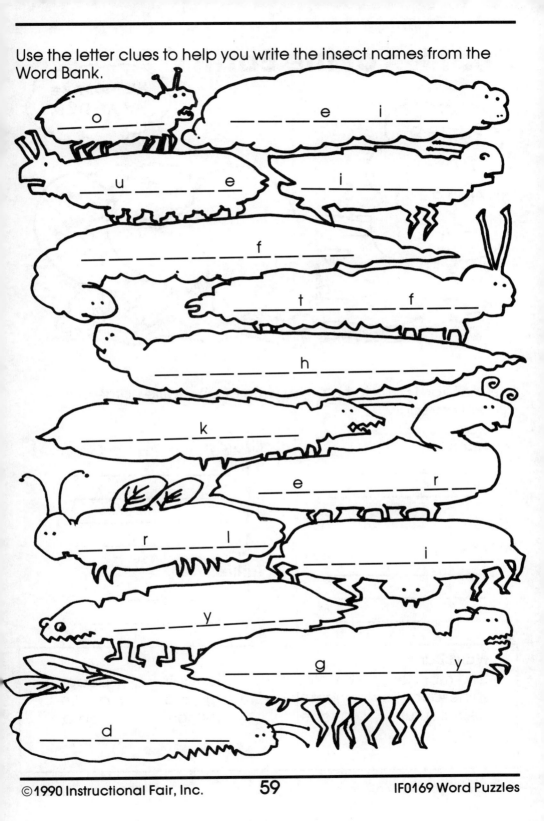

Reptiles of the Earth

Use the Word Bank to help you write each reptile name in the correct category.

Dinosaurs:
1. _____
2. _____
3. _____

Snakes:
1. _____
2. _____
3. _____

Lizards:
1. _____
2. _____
3. _____
4. _____

Turtles:
1. _____
2. _____

Word Bank

Gila monster	brontosaurus	terrapin	adder
spinosaurus	chameleon	iguana	gecko
stegosaurus	tortoise	python	cobra

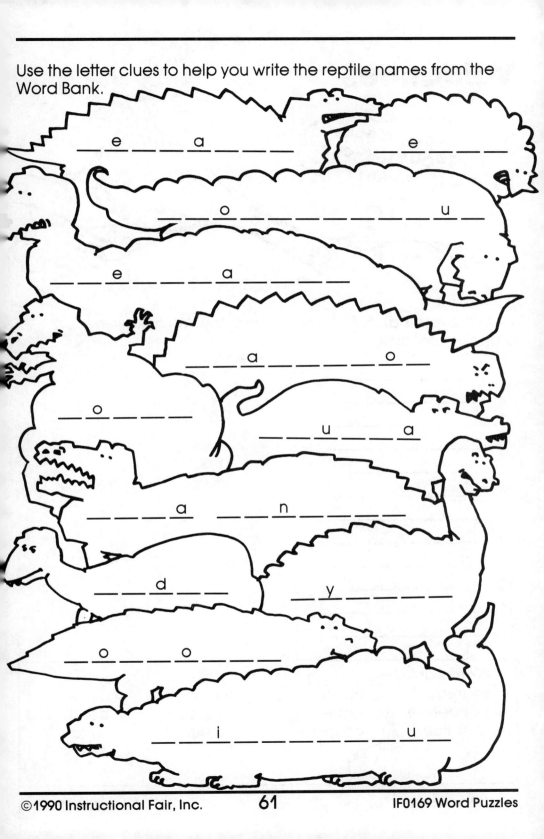

Volcanoes

Write the terms about volcanoes from the Word Bank in alphabetical order.

1. _____
2. _____
3. _____
4. _____
5. _____
6. _____
7. _____
8. _____
9. _____
10. _____
11. _____
12. _____

Word Bank

seamount	fissure	pumice	cinder
pahoehoe	crater	magma	bombs
obsidian	caldera	geyser	dyke

Use the letter clues to help you write the terms from the Word Bank.

Light

Use the Word Bank to help you unscramble the following terms about light.

1. nneo _____
2. tmnealif _____
3. ntoicfarer _____
4. feelrtcnoi _____
5. rlsea maeb _____
6. npooht _____
7. htlnegewva _____
8. mrsip _____
9. rrdaa _____
10. ocirmsveaw _____
11. odiar vseaw _____
12. mturcpes _____

Word Bank

microwaves	laser beam	spectrum	prism
radio waves	refraction	filament	radar
wavelength	reflection	photon	neon

Use the letter clues to help you write the terms about light from the Word Bank.

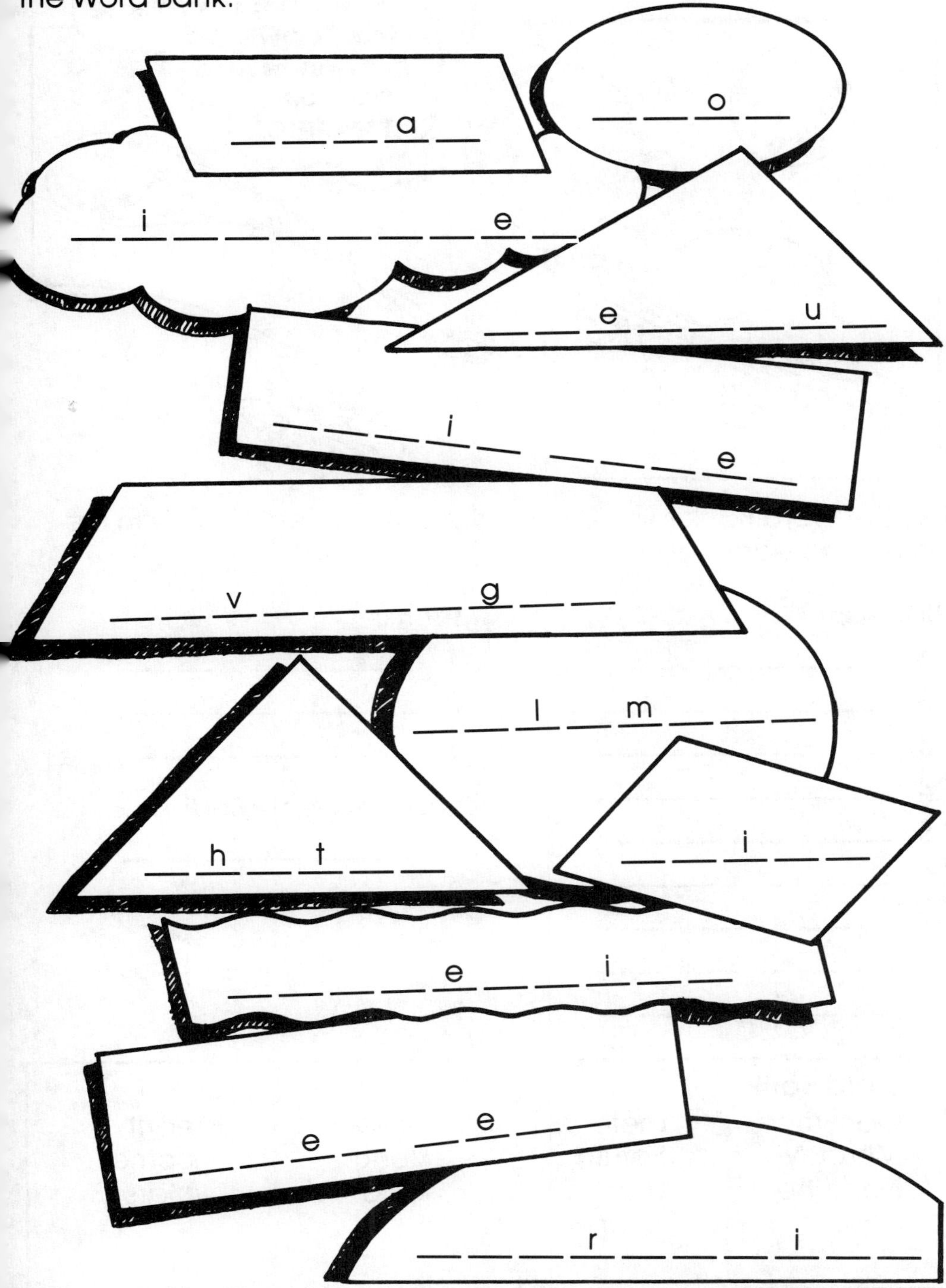

_ _ _ a _ _ _

_ _ _ _ o _

_ i _ _ _ _ _ _ _ _ e _ _

_ _ _ e _ _ _ _ u _

_ _ _ _ i _ _ _ _ _ _ _ e

_ _ v _ _ _ _ g _ _ _ _ _

_ _ _ _ l _ m _ _ _ _

_ h _ t _ _ _

_ _ _ _ _ i _ _

_ _ _ _ _ e _ _ i _ _

_ _ e _ _ e _ _ _

_ _ _ _ _ r _ _ _ i _

Celestial Bodies

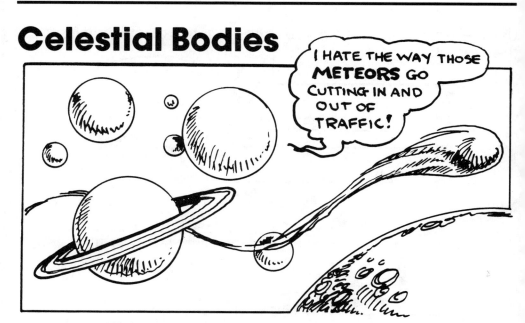

Use the Word Bank to help you write each celestial body in the correct category.

Planets:
1. _____
2. _____
3. _____
4. _____
5. _____
6. _____
7. _____
8. _____
9. _____

Moons:
1. _____
2. _____
3. _____

Other Heavenly Bodies:
1. _____
2. _____

Word Bank

Ganymede	meteor	Phobos	earth
Mercury	Saturn	Venus	comet
Neptune	Uranus	Pluto	Mars
Jupiter	Triton		

Use the Word Bank to help you add vowels to each of these solar system terms.

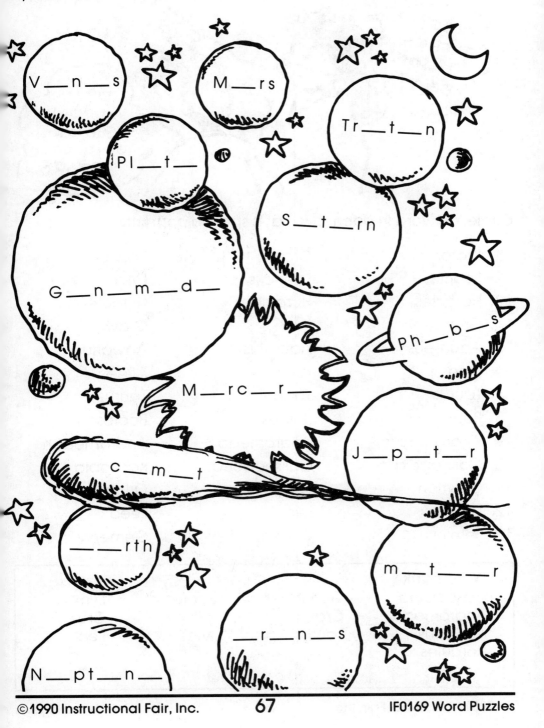

Constellations

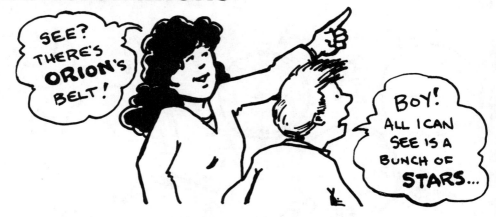

Circle the word in each row that is spelled correctly.

1. Krator — Crater — Kreyter
2. Leenks — Leencks — Lynx
3. Hercules — Hurqulees — Hurculees
4. Crux — Krux — Crawx
5. Aquereus — Aquarius — Aqwarius
6. Erees — Aries — Airees
7. Taurus — Torus — Tauruz
8. Bouts — Boutes — Bootes
9. Andramada — Andromeda — Andramedah
10. Cassiopeia — Casseopeea — Kassiopia
11. Ohwrion — Owrion — Orion
12. Lio — Leo — Leeo
13. Jemini — Gemini — Gemeniy

Word Bank
Cassiopeia, Gemini, Bootes, Lynx
Andromeda, Crater, Orion, Crux
Aquarius, Taurus, Aries, Leo
Hercules

Use the Word Bank to help you add vowels to each of these constellations.

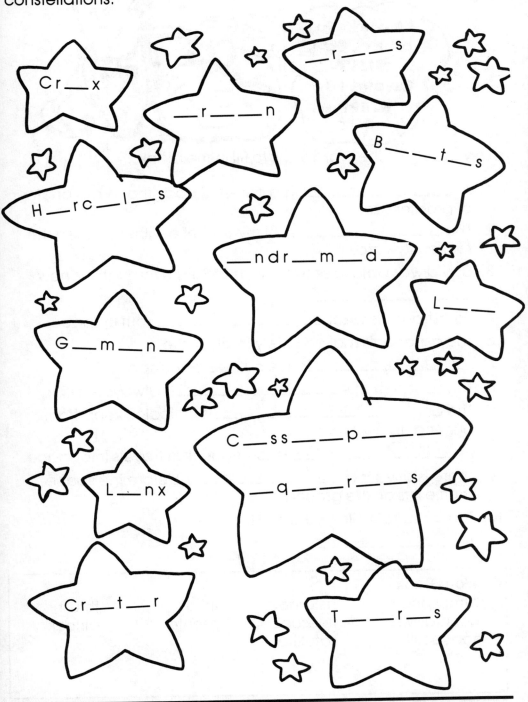

Space Travel

Use words from the Word Bank to fill in the blanks.

1. A _____ is a celestial body that orbits another of greater size.
2. The _____ of the rocket engines pushed the rocket skyward.
3. David was able to see the rings of Saturn through his new _____.
4. All astronauts wear a _____ out in space.
5. The astronauts moved safely through the _____ to the outside of the spaceship.
6. The space shuttle _____ is always exciting!
7. The angle of _____ is critical to keep from burning up.
8. An _____ is someone that travels into space.
9. There is always a _____ before the space shuttle lifts off the ground.
10. The air surrounding a planet is called its _____.

Word Bank
atmosphere   astronaut   lift-off   thrust
countdown   telescope   reentry   airlock
spacesuit   satellite

Use the Word Bank to help you add vowels to each of these space terms.

The Space Shuttle

Write the space shuttle terms from the Word Bank in alphabetical order.

1. _____
2. _____
3. _____
4. _____
5. _____
6. _____
7. _____

Word Bank

deployment   cargo bay
main engines   orbiter   spaceport
flight deck   launch pad

Use the key to help you decode the following terms about the space shuttle. The Word Bank will help you.

1.

2.

3.

4.

5.

6.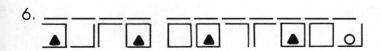

7.

Computers

Write the syllables for each computer term in the spaces provided.

1. printout _____ _____
2. cursor _____ _____
3. compatible _____ _____ _____ _____
4. search _____
5. hardware _____ _____
6. malfunction _____ _____ _____
7. program _____ _____
8. font _____

Word Bank
malfunction   printout   cursor   search
compatible   hardware   font
               program

Use the key to help you decode the following computer terms. The Word Bank will help you.

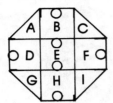 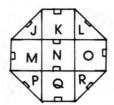 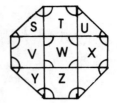

1.

2.

3.

4.

5.

6.

7.

8.

Computers

Write the syllables for each computer term in the spaces provided.

1. byte _____

2. output _____ _____

3. access _____ _____

4. escape _____ _____

5. memory _____ _____ _____

6. glitch _____

7. input _____ _____

8. retrieval _____ _____ _____

Word Bank
retrieval   output   glitch   byte
access   input   memory
escape

Use the key to help you decode the following computer terms. The Word Bank will help you.

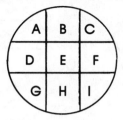 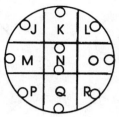 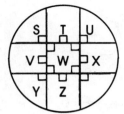

1.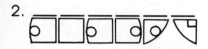

2.

Polygons

 A. B. C. D.

E. 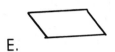 F. G. H.

I. J. K.  L.

Match each polygon with its geometric shape.

_____ 1. trapezoid
_____ 2. rhombus
_____ 3. parallelogram
_____ 4. pyramid
_____ 5. rectangle
_____ 6. decagon
_____ 7. heptagon
_____ 8. triangle
_____ 9. quadrilateral
_____ 10. pentagon
_____ 11. octagon
_____ 12. nonagon

Word Bank
quadrilateral   rectangle   decagon   triangle
parallelogram   rhombus   heptagon   octagon
trapezoid   pyramid   pentagon   nonagon

Decode the names of geometric shapes from the Word Bank by finding a letter of the alphabet that stands for each number. One is done for you.

$\overset{t}{11}\ \overset{r}{9}\ \overset{i}{26}\ \overset{a}{18}\ \overset{n}{5}\ \overset{g}{24}\ \overset{l}{3}\ \overset{e}{22}$

$\overline{6}\ \overline{20}\ \overline{11}\ \overline{18}\ \overline{24}\ \overline{6}\ \overline{5}$

$\overline{25}\ \overline{22}\ \overline{7}\ \overline{11}\ \overline{18}\ \overline{24}\ \overline{6}\ \overline{5}$

$\overline{11}\ \overline{9}\ \overline{18}\ \overline{7}\ \overline{22}\ \overline{17}\ \overline{6}\ \overline{26}\ \overline{21}$

$\overline{7}\ \overline{16}\ \overline{9}\ \overline{18}\ \overline{4}\ \overline{26}\ \overline{21}$

$\overline{7}\ \overline{22}\ \overline{5}\ \overline{11}\ \overline{18}\ \overline{24}\ \overline{6}\ \overline{5}$

$\overline{5}\ \overline{6}\ \overline{5}\ \overline{18}\ \overline{24}\ \overline{6}\ \overline{5}$

$\overline{9}\ \overline{25}\ \overline{6}\ \overline{4}\ \overline{19}\ \overline{12}\ \overline{10}$

$\overline{21}\ \overline{22}\ \overline{20}\ \overline{18}\ \overline{24}\ \overline{6}\ \overline{5}$

$\overline{9}\ \overline{22}\ \overline{20}\ \overline{11}\ \overline{18}\ \overline{5}\ \overline{24}\ \overline{3}\ \overline{22}$

$\overline{8}\ \overline{12}\ \overline{18}\ \overline{21}\ \overline{9}\ \overline{26}\ \overline{3}\ \overline{18}\ \overline{11}\ \overline{22}\ \overline{9}\ \overline{18}\ \overline{3}$

$\overline{7}\ \overline{18}\ \overline{9}\ \overline{18}\ \overline{3}\ \overline{3}\ \overline{22}\ \overline{3}\ \overline{6}\ \overline{24}\ \overline{9}\ \overline{18}\ \overline{4}$

Mathematics

Circle the word in each row that is spelled correctly.

1. vayreable / vaireable / variable
2. reciprocals / resipracles / resiprecles
3. kwoshent / cwoshint / quotient
4. praportion / proportion / proporshon
5. probability / prawbabilaty / prabawbilatee
6. maltapels / multiples / mulltaples
7. frakshun / frackshon / fraction
8. percent / pursent / purcent
9. davisor / divisor / daviser
10. bysect / bisect / biseckt
11. kungrewent / kungruent / congruent
12. divadend / divadened / dividend
13. estamait / estimate / estamate
14. perimeter / purimater / purematur

Word Bank
probability   multiples   variable   percent
reciprocals   congruent   quotient   divisor
proportion   dividend   fraction   bisect
perimeter   estimate

Decode the math terms from the Word Bank by finding a letter of the alphabet that stands for each number. One is done for you.

v a r i a b l e
5 26 9 18 26 25 15 22

q u o t i e n t
10 6 12 7 18 22 13 7

f r a c t i o n
21 9 26 24 7 18 12 13

p r o b a b i l i t y
11 9 12 25 26 25 18 15 18 7 2

m u l t i p l e s
14 6 15 7 18 11 15 22 8

c o n g r u e n t
24 12 13 20 9 6 22 13 7

p e r i m e t e r
11 22 9 18 14 22 7 22 9

e s t i m a t e
22 8 7 18 14 26 7 22

d i v i d e n d
23 18 5 18 23 22 13 23

p r o p o r t i o n
11 9 12 11 12 9 7 18 12 13

r e c i p r o c a l s
9 22 24 18 11 9 12 24 26 15 8

b i s e c t
25 18 8 22 24 7

d i v i s o r
23 18 5 18 8 12 9

p e r c e n t
11 22 9 24 22 13 7

Mathematic Terms

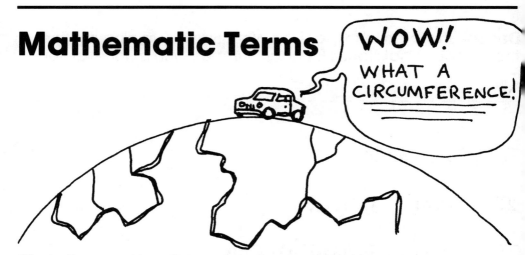

Circle the word in each row that is spelled correctly.

1. prawduckt — product — praduct
2. entagur — integer — entager
3. sematre — sematry — symmetry
4. purpendiculer — purpindikulur — perpendicular
5. vurhtex — vurtex — vertex
6. capacity — capasity — capasaty
7. circumference — sirkumfurence — sircumfurance
8. equation — ekwasion — ecwasion
9. dyagonal — diagunel — diagonal
10. diamutur — diameter — dyamater
11. xponunt — exponent — exponant
12. hipotanoose — hypotinoose — hypotenuse
13. factor — faktur — facktur
14. desimal — decimal — desamull

Word Bank
circumference equation product vertex
perpendicular diagonal decimal factor
hypotenuse diameter capacity integer
symmetry exponent

Decode the following list of math terms from the Word Bank by finding a letter of the alphabet that stands for each number. One is done for you.

$\overset{c}{23}\ \overset{i}{3}\ \overset{r}{12}\ \overset{c}{23}\ \overset{u}{15}\ \overset{m}{7}\ \overset{f}{26}\ \overset{e}{25}\ \overset{r}{12}\ \overset{e}{25}\ \overset{n}{8}\ \overset{c}{23}\ \overset{e}{25}$

$\overline{2}\ \overline{19}\ \overline{10}\ \overline{9}\ \overline{14}\ \overline{25}\ \overline{8}\ \overline{15}\ \overline{13}\ \overline{25}$

$\overline{10}\ \overline{25}\ \overline{12}\ \overline{10}\ \overline{25}\ \overline{8}\ \overline{24}\ \overline{3}\ \overline{23}\ \overline{15}\ \overline{6}\ \overline{21}\ \overline{12}$

$\overline{13}\ \overline{19}\ \overline{7}\ \overline{7}\ \overline{25}\ \overline{14}\ \overline{12}\ \overline{19}$

$\overline{16}\ \overline{25}\ \overline{12}\ \overline{14}\ \overline{25}\ \overline{18}$

$\overline{24}\ \overline{25}\ \overline{23}\ \overline{3}\ \overline{7}\ \overline{21}\ \overline{6}$

$\overline{3}\ \overline{8}\ \overline{14}\ \overline{25}\ \overline{1}\ \overline{25}\ \overline{12}$

$\overline{25}\ \overline{18}\ \overline{10}\ \overline{9}\ \overline{8}\ \overline{25}\ \overline{8}\ \overline{14}$

$\overline{24}\ \overline{3}\ \overline{21}\ \overline{1}\ \overline{9}\ \overline{8}\ \overline{21}\ \overline{6}$

$\overline{25}\ \overline{11}\ \overline{15}\ \overline{21}\ \overline{14}\ \overline{3}\ \overline{9}\ \overline{8}$

$\overline{10}\ \overline{12}\ \overline{9}\ \overline{24}\ \overline{15}\ \overline{23}\ \overline{14}$

$\overline{26}\ \overline{21}\ \overline{23}\ \overline{14}\ \overline{9}\ \overline{12}$

$\overline{24}\ \overline{3}\ \overline{21}\ \overline{7}\ \overline{25}\ \overline{14}\ \overline{25}\ \overline{12}$

$\overline{23}\ \overline{21}\ \overline{10}\ \overline{21}\ \overline{23}\ \overline{3}\ \overline{14}\ \overline{19}$

More great workbooks for grade level 6 from Instructional Fair

Teacher-developed and classroom-tested workbooks that make you "the expert" when it comes to helping your child in the basic skills areas.

These workbooks (8½" x 10½") contain 54 pages of activities that your child can do independently. A pull-out answer key is also included for easy correcting.

Math Skills Workbook
Level 6

- Addition and Subtraction
- Multiplication and Division
- Fractions
- Decimals
- Measurement
- Word Problems
  plus more . . .

IF0506 Math Skills 6

Reading Skills Workbook
Level 6

- Following Directions
- Sequencing
- Vocabulary
- Using the Context
- Thinking Skills
- Research Skills
  plus more . . .

IF0512 Reading Skills 6

PLEASE RETURN TO:
MRS. TRACY FUNDERBURK

Comprehension Skills Workbook
Level 6

- Finding the Main Idea
- Reading for Details
- Sequencing
- Reading for Understanding
  plus more . . .

IF0518 Comprehension Skills 6

Language Skills Workbook
Level 6

- Nouns and Pronouns
- Adjectives and Adverbs
- Spelling
- Types of Sentences
- Punctuation
- Prepositions
  plus more . . .

IF0524 Language Skills 6

Learning Skills Workbook
Level 6

- Following Directions
- Research Skills
- Sequencing
- Comprehension
- Fractions
- Vocabulary
  plus more . . .

IF0530 Learning Skills 6

Writing Skills Workbook
Level 6

- Expanding Sentences
- Combining Sentences
- Proofreading
- Using Notes and Outlines
- Writing Poetry
  plus more . . .

IF0536 Writing Skills 6

©1990, Instructional Fair, Inc.